The Mystery of Discipleship

A 91 Day Epic Voyage as a Disciple

The Mystery of Discipleship

A 91 Day Epic Voyage as a Disciple

By
Martha Kilpatrick

Shulamite Ministries
SUCHES, GEORGIA

ISBN-13 978-1-936057-35-1
ISBN-10 1-936057-35-2

The Mystery of Discipleship

Shulamite Ministries
PO Box 10
Suches, GA 30572
www.shulamite.com
888-355-5373
info@shulamite.com

Statement of Faith

Jesus Christ, the only begotten Son of God,
came in the flesh, shed His holy Blood on the
Cross at Calvary for the sins of the world.
He is Lord of the Universe, King of Kings...

and I am His Shulamite.

I will praise You, O Lord, with my whole heart;
I will show forth
(recount and tell aloud)
all Your marvelous works and wonderful deeds!
Psalm 9:1 AMPC

Foreword

The Mystery of Discipleship was not written for those who consider themselves to be wise, noble, or ample. They would never pay the actual price it costs to be a disciple. Capable men and women are satisfied with themselves and what they have accomplished. A disciple, on the other hand, comes to the table with nothing but a YES to Jesus!

The Mystery of Discipleship is a 91-day epic voyage for the disciple. Who is the disciple? A disciple is one at the end of his rope. A disciple has come up empty while yearning for more. A disciple has nowhere else to turn. These are the men and women who will abandon all to embrace all of Him.

Are you one of the foolish and weak Christ has chosen? Come and experience the adventure of Life.

John Enslow

Introduction

I would like to introduce myself. Really...introduce my *self*.

Growing up, my family lived in a wonderful stone house in the country. There were no other children near us, so from 4 to 8 years old, I really was alone.

I have always called myself a little scared rabbit. In myself I am shy and reticent and love being alone. I loved my child-world of woods, creeks, and my brown and white pinto pony.

I didn't like to be seen or noticed. My mother tried to cure that by giving me elocution lessons around the age of 7 (elocution: the skill of clear and expressive speech).

I had to learn delightful short poems and then recite them from memory in front of an audience. I learned to enjoy it. Little did I know I was rehearsing for the future! And I came to see it wasn't so terrible. But after the 'performance' I would go back to the woods and trails of my rabbit world.

Alone. I loved being alone, sitting on the ground and gazing at the distant mountains of Tennessee. My world was quiet so I was quiet and contemplative, even as a child. I lived in books and nature. And my parents let me be. I wasn't really afraid of life, I was just very shy.

When I radically encountered Jesus in my 20s, I was a church-goer but I knew not one born-again Christian. So my nature was perfectly content to be alone with just Jesus!

As I lived in my Bible – Matthew, Mark, Luke, and John (no other parts of the Bible yet) – I felt that if you knew Christ then you were automatically a disciple. And I assumed what the disciples did was simply the norm and

I should live as they lived. So I followed their example. When they prayed for healing, I prayed for healing, and there were healings because I simply believed in healing. They heard God speak, so I expected to hear God myself…and so I did. As they obeyed the Lord, I knew the relationship with Christ was all about obedience. So I said to Him many times, "Whatever You tell me I will obey."

When He clearly called me to be a writer, it was the most terrible of possibilities. That call struck at my deep love of solitude and required it to die. I didn't want to be famous, I didn't want my little private thoughts, my quiet inner world, spread out for others to inspect and judge!

It so went against my nature that I feared I would refuse the whole idea as not-God. But I really knew it was God. So I quickly said, "YES, LORD." Immediately I searched and found a seminar for would-be Christian writers in Dallas, Texas. I got on a plane and went to that 3-day seminar. The Author met me gloriously there in Dallas and so began the process of becoming what I was meant to be.

I have told the whole story elsewhere. But I tell some of it now for your sake, dear reader. I entered the journey not knowing the cost of following Jesus. This book will show you the cost, the reward…*and* the final glory.

I was to learn in life and from writers like Andrew Murray, Watchman Nee and Austin-Sparks that there is a difference between a believer and a disciple. Not everyone who is born again, will be a disciple of Christ. There is a giant IF-gate you have to squeeze through.

Such is Father's integrity that He never hides the reality of your calling. It's all there in the Book. The terms of His call to discipleship are stark and costly. I don't spare the reader in this book. I 'tell it like it is.' The path of a *true* disciple is tough and wonderful, frightening and fascinating. It is an adventure not to be missed.

This book is really *for* the fainthearted, the scared, the shy, such as I have been. In answer to my 'yes' in the face of a great dread of being an author, the Lord took over my voyage and carried me through paths of wilderness, lions, dangers and along the way, many green shelters for shy rabbits... It was a completely perfect sail.

I was forced to need to be transformed into a completely different person. And then I discovered that my Author had already accomplished that! I merely took off the robe of the scared rabbit and put on Christ Himself (Ephesians 4:22f). How amazing!

But I was to find in writing about this Wonderful Counselor, the greatest joy and delight I could ever know.

Fullness and bliss are where you are headed, Disciple! I don't spare you but I will by the Spirit put you on a little boat for this voyage and you will find yourself being carried away by Him, to Him. You will live the book of your own story of Christ, a living epistle, read by those He sends to know you.

There will be books and books in heaven. Your story will be written. Take courage, all is ready for you to sail high above a common life and into the heavenly realms. In this life!

Oh, and by the way, writing is my greatest and hardest adventure and . . . my sweetest fulfillment. What do you know! I was meant to be what I never was nor wanted to be.

So God can point to us in all future ages as examples
of the incredible wealth of his grace and kindness toward us,
as shown in all he has done for us who are united with Christ
Jesus.

For we are God's masterpiece.
He has created us anew in Christ Jesus,
so we can do the good things He planned for us long ago.
Ephesians 2:7, 10 NLT

You are a masterpiece in process. Be clay on the Potter's wheel and you will never imagine what He will invest *in you* and make *of you*.

The Lord of all can handle any scared rabbit.

DAY 1

A Disciple Can Make Disciples

Matthew 28:19-20 ESV
Go then and make disciples of all the nations, baptizing them
in the name of the Father and of the Son and of the Holy Spirit,
teaching them to observe everything that I have commanded you.
And behold, I am with you…

Jesus spoke this command to disciples. Not the crowds, not believers. To the disciples only.

There is a difference between a believer and a disciple.

Only a disciple can make disciples, and that happens by this great promise of the Lord: His presence WITH His disciples. And it is His presence that 'makes' a disciple. I cannot orchestrate a disciple, nor choose who will be one! I am often shocked by who the Lord touches, sometimes people I don't even know…or notice.

How awesome is our influence! How crucial is our discipleship! Only disciples 'make' disciples!

This great commission rests on disciples reproducing disciples. And to disciples is the earthshaking promise of the certain and unfailing presence of the Lord. The manifest presence of the Lord!

This is the heart, the power, the very *mystery* of making disciples of all nations.

Father, I have the desire to be not just a believer but Your disciple. Thank You for the call and Your faithfulness to make me a disciple. Of Jesus.

DAY 2

The Model and Order for a Disciple

Matthew 4:18-20 NASB
Now as Jesus was walking by the Sea of Galilee, He saw two
brothers, Simon who was called Peter, and Andrew his brother
casting a net into the sea; for they were fishermen. And He
said to them, "Follow Me, and I will make you fishers of
men." Immediately they left their nets and followed Him.

The fishermen had seen Jesus' miracles and heard
Him speak. He had ministered many miracles in the area
around the Sea. They did not instantly abandon their
family, home, property and livelihood for a whim. Their
hearts had already been captured, and they went by no
ambition because there was no promise of greatness.
They did not follow out of logic, as there was no time to
calculate.

"Immediately" they left all and went wherever
this One who invited led them. They joined—not
fully understanding who the Man was, not knowing
the destination, and having no concept of the future
implications of the calling. They abandoned all, simply…to
be WITH Him!

This is the model and order for a disciple. Seeing,
knowing, loving…hearing, leaving all, following blindly.
Unequivocal abandonment, holding on to nothing.

Father, please show me the places in my heart where I am still
holding on to something or someone other than You. From Jesus.

DAY 3

Discipleship Is an Offer

Luke 14:26 NASB
If anyone comes to me and does not...he cannot be My disciple.

Jesus always placed an 'if' before His conditions for discipleship. Salvation is by grace, utterly free. Discipleship is an offer that requires a decision.

It is the call of every child of God to follow Christ as disciple. It is a privilege given...but ever it is a choice.

God gives salvation. He 'makes' His children by supernatural birth from above, but you make YOURSELF a disciple.

Father, I choose YOU. I set my heart and my will on following You as Your disciple. For Jesus.

DAY 4

Honor in the Lowest Place

Let me set the stage for Jesus' "Cost of Discipleship"…

Luke 14:1, 7-11 NIV

One Sabbath, when Jesus went to eat in the house of a prominent Pharisee, He was being carefully watched.

When He noticed how the guests picked the places of honor at the table, He told them this parable: "When someone invites you to a wedding feast, do not take the place of honor, for a person more distinguished than you may have been invited. If so, the host who invited both of you will come and say to you, 'Give this person your seat.' Then, humiliated, you will have to take the least important place.

But when you are invited, take the lowest place, so that when your host comes, he will say to you, 'Friend, move up to a better place.' Then you will be honored in the presence of all the other guests. For all those who exalt themselves will be humbled, and those who humble themselves will be exalted."

Jesus' real meaning is of a far distant and higher wedding feast: the Marriage Supper of the Lamb. This is the pinnacle of human history, the culmination and reward of following the Lord in His humility and humiliation. The entire anticipation of the disciple is for that Feast. The disciple's motivation for this life is to be present and part of the Marriage of the Lamb. And the requirement for that feast is the "lowest place."

Father, I want to be at the Marriage Supper of the Lamb. Show me in my life where I can take the lowest place. I desire to be present at the Feast. By Jesus.

DAY 5

Discipleship Requires a Change of Thinking

Luke 14:12-13 NASB
And He also went on to say to the one who had invited Him,
"When you give a luncheon or a dinner, do not invite your
friends or your brothers or your relatives or rich neighbors,
otherwise they may also invite you in return and that will be
your repayment. But when you give a reception, invite the poor,
the crippled, the lame, the blind...

Jesus challenged the values of His host. The Pharisee's
choice of guests was typically human but not divinely
inspired. God's preference is the sick (Mt. 9:12), the
wounded (Lk. 10:25-37), and the poor (Mt. 5:3).

To understand discipleship, there must be a change
from human nature that welcomes the successful, the rich
and the family, which is really a selfish investment for an
immediate return. To comprehend the issue of discipleship
before God, Jesus had to effect a transformation of
thinking. It is only the needy, the unable, the poor, and the
ignorant that can become a disciple. The proud, the strong,
the independent, and the 'knowing' will not qualify.

Father, please let me see with YOUR eyes what my earthly eyes
miss. I choose to love who You love, where You love, and how
You love! Through Jesus.

DAY 6

The Truly Hungry Follow Jesus

In Luke 14, Jesus actually gave two parables. In verse 12-14, the Lord Jesus sets the stage, the call and the reward for our relationships and our outreach.

Luke 14:13 NASB
But when you give a reception, invite the poor, the crippled, the lame, the blind…

This is not merely literal. It is a picture of the needy. Those who are needy, who are "poor in spirit," who are crushed by suffering, crippled by life and unable to understand or see God rightly.

The needy…the desperate. These very ones were willing to see, recognize and follow Jesus. And these are the very ones to whom we offer the 'food of Life,' for they are the only ones who will 'eat,' because they are the truly hungry.

The strong, the mighty, the capable, the independent—these are not crippled or poor and so are not hungry.

Father, thank You for making me needy and dependent. Without my poverty, I wouldn't see You, much less follow You. To Jesus.

DAY 7

The Desire for Reward

The Pharisees invited to their banquet those who could repay them. Most of what we do is done for personal gain, yet the Lord doesn't condemn the desire for reward. He Himself offers a reward:

Luke 14:13-14 AMPC
But when you give a banquet or a reception, invite the poor, the disabled, the lame, and the blind. Then you will be blessed (happy, fortunate, and to be envied), because they have no way of repaying you, and you will be recompensed at the resurrection of the just (upright).

There are two rewards. The first is in this human life: enormous and obvious blessing. The second is a reward in the next life.

The next parable of Luke 14 reveals the "reward at the resurrection."

Father, I do desire reward and I choose the Reward You value over what the world has to offer me. Through Jesus.

DAY 8

Marriage of the Lamb

Luke 14:15-17 NASB
When one of those who were reclining at the table with Him heard this, he said to Him, "Blessed is everyone who will eat bread in the kingdom of God!"

But He said to him, "A man was giving a big dinner, and he invited many; and at the dinner hour he sent his slave to say to those who had been invited, 'Come; for everything is ready now.'"

The great finale of discipleship will be the Marriage of the Lamb. It is the Father's goal and gift to His Son. It is a real and coming event. For the disciple, the Marriage Supper is the reward of this life's struggle, the highest union with the Lord. And for that reason, it is the motivation and direction of the disciple.

The Father's goal for His Beloved Son becomes (by the work of the Spirit) the disciple's own goal and secret joy: "The Marriage of the Lamb!"

Father, do all that it takes to make the Marriage of the Lamb my heart's true motivation and desire. With Jesus.

DAY 9

When the Invitees Make Excuses

Luke 14:15-18a NASB
When one of those who were reclining at the table with Him heard this, he said to Him, "Blessed is everyone who will eat bread in the kingdom of God!"

But He said to him, "A man was giving a big dinner, and he invited many; and at the dinner hour he sent his slave to say to those who had been invited, 'Come; for everything is ready now.'"

But they all alike began to make excuses.

This man was speaking of a Messianic event, a feast to which Jews were looking.

A Jewish banquet in Jesus' day was prepared in this way: invitations were sent out and the reply was given to the host, but the time was not announced. When the supper was ready, servants would go out to notify the guests. The guests would have already agreed to attend, but in the parable when the time came, they 'made excuses.'

In part, Jesus was speaking about Jews, those first invited to the banquet—the Marriage of the Lamb. Jesus was addressing their rejection of Him. But in the larger picture He was speaking of believers as well. Those who agree to follow the Lamb in principle but in reality will also "make excuses."

Father, I lay down all my excuses. I receive Your invitation and say yes! To Jesus.

DAY 10

Possessions, Position, and People

Luke 14:18-20 ESV
But they all alike began to make excuses. The first said to him 'I have bought a field and I must go out and see it. Please have me excused.'

And another said, 'I have bought five yoke of oxen, and I go to examine them. Please have me excused.'

And another said, 'I have married a wife, and therefore I cannot come.'

These three stand for those invited-believers who prefer worldly life to divine culmination. The three areas of human entanglements are Possessions, Position, and People.

The first was occupied with the ownership of property. His roots and joys were in the earth. The second was concerned with his position in the world. The ox speaks of power and dominion. And the third put his wife, his love-relationship, above God.

You cannot love the world in daily preoccupation and see the Banquet when the time comes. The great Feast of the Lamb is to be anticipated and chosen, the joyful objective of this common life.

Father, I relinquish all my human entanglements and my daily preoccupation with the love of the world. For You are my joyful Reward always! In Jesus.

DAY 11

The Difference Between Disciples and Believers

1 John 2:15-17 ESV
Do not love the world or the things in the world. If anyone loves
the world, the love of the Father is not in him. For all that is
in the world – the desires of the flesh and the desires of the eye
and pride in possession – is not from the Father but is from the
world. And the world is passing away along with its desires, but
whoever does the will of God abides forever.

The three excuses of the parable were desires of the flesh
(the man with the wife), the desires of the eye (the man
who wanted to see his land), and the pride of possession
(the man who would see his oxen). It's all a question of
what you focus on to SEE, to keep before you, to think and
dwell on…because what you focus on is what you love.

This was a not an issue of work or responsibility but
entirely a matter of LOVE. What you love holds you,
occupies you, and is your motivation. So to choose your
possessions, your position, or your people is actually love
of the world and exposes that the love of the Father is not
in you.

The core and hidden difference between disciples and
believers is simply…LOVE. It is not the degree of service,
the right doctrines, vast knowledge, or great achievement
that makes a disciple. It is only LOVE.

The believer has Jesus. The disciple *loves* Jesus.

Father, show me what I focus on and what I truly love. For I
desire that love for YOU hold me, occupy me, and motivate me.
Through Jesus.

DAY 12

Guests of the Marriage Supper

The Parable of the Great Banquet points to the Marriage Supper of the Lamb. Those who were invited made excuses and the host responded.

Luke 14:21 ESV
So the servant came and reported these things to his master. Then the master of the house became angry and said to his servant, 'Go out quickly to the streets and lanes of the city, and bring in the poor and crippled and blind and lame.'

Those who have their joys in this life are invited. The feast is not exclusive! It is INCLUSIVE of all, but only the ones who anticipate this eternal event will hear the call.

The poor, the needy, the dependent—these are the ones who will attend. The needy pursued Jesus. The poor in spirit will be the guests and will accept the invitation.

Father, I confess that I am needy and dependent, and I accept Your glorious invitation to be Your guest at the Marriage Supper. For Jesus.

DAY 13

What Is God's View of Disciples?

The parable of the "Great Feast" is a preparation for Jesus' most extensive discourse about discipleship. The story holds the secrets of God's view of disciples.

Luke 14:21 ESV
So the servant came and reported these things to his master. Then the master of the house became angry and said to his servant, 'Go out quickly to the streets and lanes of the city, and bring in the poor and crippled and blind and lame.'

We are all born with Adamic independence, and the world system encourages human strength. So the strong will not need the Lord. The self-sufficient never would bow to enter. The ambitious will not care to attend. The worldly will not follow Christ. And the religious will not *want* to attend!

Only the needy, the weak and the poor sought out the Lord when He walked here. He never knocked on doors. He never invaded and truly, He never begged anyone to follow Him.

Jesus offered. He invited. But the response is yours...and mine.

Father, please show me my self-sufficiency and independence of You, that I might fully and joyfully accept Your invitation. In Jesus.

DAY 14

Utter Dependence: Blind, Poor, Lame, and Needy

Luke 14:22-24 ESV
And the servant said, 'Sir, what you commanded has been done,
and still there is room.' And the master said to the servant, 'Go
out to the highways and hedges and compel people to come in,
that my house may be filled. For I tell you, none of those men
who were invited shall taste my banquet.'

The poor, the crippled, the lame, and the blind – all who are needy by a desperate need. All who cannot survive, live or function without God's entire involvement in their lives! These know God, love God and are His disciples.

Saul persecuted the early Christians with strength and determination. He was strong in his ability, firm in his religion, and self-sufficient in his knowledge. On the 'highway' to Damascus, the Lord interrupted him and in one moment changed him from a mighty warrior fighting the wrong battle to a blind, stumbling, ignorant man. God reduced him to need – dependence on Him and on God's choice of a disciple to help him. Need of God and need of the man God sends.

Then the Lord isolated him for three years in the desert and Paul emerged as one of the greatest disciples and the one entrusted with writing epistles to all believers through the ages and into eternity. And Paul boasted of his weakness, loved his dependence, taught the early church – and us – to live as he lived: in vulnerability and total need of God (2 Corinthians 12:8-10).

Paul is the great picture of God's ability to produce the necessary need that enables us to fall to the ground before Him…and how He can compel a man on the road to his own destruction to come to His feast!

Father, thank You for reducing me to need and vulnerability,
that I may meet You and know You in my complete dependence
on You! In Jesus.

DAY 15

How a Believer Becomes a Disciple

Luke 14:25-26 NIV
Large crowds were traveling with Jesus, and turning to them He said, "If anyone comes to Me and does not hate his father and mother, his wife and children, his brothers and sisters – yes, even his own life – he cannot be My disciple."

From the Banquet of the Lamb, Jesus turned to present the way into the banquet and the picture of those who will be seated at the table of His joy.

Jesus gives the first condition by which a believer becomes a disciple. As Lord, He asks first place in love before any of our most treasured relationships, our closest ties on earth. Only in this condition can a believer become the disciple of His intimacy.

This is stated as a condition of discipleship – the most severe condition because 'disciple' is above all about relationship with Christ, not service and not human relationships. The disciple lives for and from a private love relationship. Any service or obedience is not the focus or the objective…but the RESULT of following the Lamb.

Therefore, a Christian can be a great leader and not qualify as a disciple. A Christian can be a preacher, missionary, prophet – and never become a disciple.

Father, I choose to give You first place. I will love You above ALL others, with all my heart, with all my soul, with all my mind, and with all my strength. Through Jesus.

DAY 16

The IF of Discipleship

Luke 14:26 NIV
If anyone comes to Me and does not hate his father and mother,
his wife and children, his brothers and sisters — yes even his own
life — he cannot be My disciple.

This verse does not bear the imperative of a command. It is laid out as an option. The great "IF" at the beginning means this must be a conscious decision out of a chosen preference for the Lord. This requirement for a disciple is purely choice... You do not have to obey this to be a Christian. We are saved by grace alone. But discipleship is the ultimate pathway, the highest calling, and it is yours and mine to embrace if we desire.

Remember that the previous parable reveals that ALL believers are invited. This is not a private club, an exclusive group especially chosen. It is an offer which any believer may refuse and any believer may embrace.

The disciples stood in an entirely different relationship to Jesus than followers, and those who *called* themselves disciples.

The disciples alone were privy to the secrets of Jesus.

The disciples could ask any question of Him and receive an answer. The disciples lived with Him, day and night. They saw Him live, pray, heal and teach. Some had the privilege of dinner with Him once but the disciples had every meal with Him for three years! They "beheld His glory" firsthand.

The disciple knows the Lord intimately, "firsthand" — knows His mind, His direction, His meaning, His Kingdom secrets.

Matthew 13:10-11, 16 NIV
The disciples came to Him and asked, "Why do You speak to the people in parables?"

He replied, "Because the knowledge of the secrets of the kingdom of heaven has been given to you, but not to them."

"But blessed are your eyes because they see, and your ears because they hear."

Father, I make the conscious decision for YOU. I will live with You day and night in intimate knowledge of YOU. By Jesus.

DAY 17

The Major Condition of Discipleship

Luke 14:26 NIV
If anyone comes to Me and does not hate his father and mother,
his wife and children, his brothers and sisters — yes even his own
life — he cannot be My disciple.

You can be a teacher yet not a disciple. You can have any ministry and yet not be a disciple. The condition for discipleship is not education, revelation, brilliance or sacrifice — not even anointing. The major condition of discipleship is to 'hate' father, mother, sister, brother, wife and children.

Only to the disciples was given the authority of power: healing, deliverance, and miracles. Only disciples were that small group of 120, who were able to be in such union of prayer that the Holy Spirit could fall upon them all. Only disciples could possibly BE in such union for those long days of prayer and waiting.

It was the disciples who wrote for Jesus, about Him.

Only His intimate disciples were trusted to speak for Him and tell His story to us. And…only disciples are commissioned to 'make disciples of all nations.'

John's epistle ends this way (21:24-25): *"This is the disciple who testifies to these things and who wrote them down. We know that his testimony is true. Jesus did many other things as well. I suppose that even the whole world would not have room for the books that would be written."*

The disciple experiences his own living history of Christ, entire books of things Jesus did in his life…

Father, please illuminate this condition of discipleship – to forsake all others – in my life. For Jesus.

DAY 18

When We Come to Christ as a Disciple

Luke 14:26 NIV
If anyone comes to Me and does not hate his father and mother,
his wife and children, his brothers and sisters — yes even his own
life — he cannot be My disciple.

This verse has perplexed commentators for centuries.
Jesus, who was Love and commanded love…and honor for
parents — how could He say this?

Most commentators say the same thing: that Jesus meant
by comparison to love for Him, it must be as far away as
hate for these family ties. They interpret it as a matter of
comparing loves. But the word used is unmistakable. The
word hate is *'miseo'* and it means to "hate, detest and even
persecute." All the major translations have to use the word
'hate' and it is called "an old and very strong word" in the
Greek. The word cannot be softened. The Holy Spirit wrote
this statement as shocking to our loyalties and bondages
to family. But it cannot be used as an excuse for malice,
bitterness or ill treatment of these family ties.

The heart of this scripture is *"If anyone comes to*
Me…" Come to Christ and, over time, this mandate
unfolds to the disciple. The one who comes to Him in
relationship and surrender will face this challenge from
the Lord. Only the Holy Spirit can orchestrate the timing
and reveal the delicate obedience to this radical loyalty to
Christ. There is a way to see this command in scripture…

Father, I come to You, and in relationship and surrender I seek to
follow the Spirit into this radical loyalty to You. In Jesus.

DAY 19

Belonging to God: A Right of Ownership

There are relationship-roles that make the strongest claim of ownership and that presume a right to dominate a disciple. I believe it is this control and right of ownership that we are to hate (not the person as such), because of an absolute loyalty to and extreme zeal for the Lord that comes only from the Spirit. To understand it, I believe that Jesus lived and demonstrated His own command. As in any of Christ's words, we look to Him for the understanding the Spirit gives...

The first recorded life incident of Jesus was at the age of twelve (Luke 2:41-52). While in Jerusalem with His family for Passover, Jesus simply walked away from His family and went to the temple. Being in a caravan, His family traveled for a day before they realized He was missing. They had to travel back to Jerusalem and it took three days to find Him in the temple, *"sitting among the teachers, listening to them and asking them questions."*

"His mother said to Him, 'Son, why have you treated us like this?'"

Mary was viewing His actions as they affected HER, and she was not trying to understand His actions as they concerned Jesus. She was claiming Him as HER son, her charge, her property. She demanded (as a natural mother would) that Jesus consider her first in His actions. Jesus' answer is astonishing because He refutes her right to His choice of direction and accepts no responsibility for the parent's anguish! He even begins to correct her. A boy of 12! Jesus protested her right of ownership over Him. He did not now BELONG to her, but to the Father.

He expected her to have known Who He belonged to –

the Father – and where He "HAD" to be — *in His Father's house*. From Jesus' view, she had been the one in the wrong, and He called her to be aware and in tune with the will of God concerning Him! He called her to go beyond natural motherhood and into the spiritual understanding that the Holy Spirit gives. His independence of her was to have been her freedom as well.

"Why were you searching for Me?" He asked. "Didn't you know I had to be in My Father's house?"

Father, I belong to Jesus and I thank You for this perfect place of belonging. To Jesus.

DAY 20

Spiritual Understanding Is Responsibility

Luke 2:49-50 AMPC
And He said to them, 'How is it that you had to look for Me?
Did you not see and know that it is necessary [as a duty] for Me
to be in My Father's house and [occupied] about My Father's
business?' But they did not comprehend what He was saying to
them.

This is frankly an incredible attitude. We know that it
is the perfect response because our Lord is perfect and
obeyed only His Father. He was led by the will of God to
the temple that day to astound the teachers there. He made
no apology for what was His obedience! The repercussions
of His obedience were not His concern.

The scripture makes note of this: *"they did not*
understand." But that was not acceptable for the two who
knew Jesus' identity. They needed to 'comprehend' Him…
to understand the will of God and spend the time to do
so. Their anguish was their own fault, and Jesus seemed
to have no sympathy for it! They should have known Who
owned Him, what His purpose was to be, and the timing
of it.

Spiritual understanding is the real role of all parents,
siblings, spouses, and sons and daughters: to hear God
for each other.

This God-given 'understanding' is so rare as to seem
merely an ideal, but God's best is for us to know each other
according to His view, His insight. And He is willing to
reveal it.

I remember an interview with Joy Dawson, the great
intercessor with YWAM. Her host asked her to define a
husband's role for a Christian wife. She answered that

he should give her absolute freedom to follow God and support whatever the Holy Spirit led her to do. The host was a bit shocked and admitted that he didn't give his own wife such liberty.

Father, I am committed to the will of the Spirit to belong to You. Now I release all those I love. Forgive me for confining them in any role. Through Jesus.

DAY 21

Christ's Dominion Isn't Cruel to Family

Luke 14:26 NIV
If anyone comes to Me and does not hate his father and mother,
his wife and children, his brothers and sisters — yes even his own
life — he cannot be My disciple.

Christ alone could obey this in perfect balance, and
Christ within you walks this out in real life, in God's
timing and His ways.

Many negate this verse by believing it is cruel to
family, to whom Christ called us to love. They believe it
contradicts His other commands. What we cannot know
until we obey the Lord when He calls for this, is that it is
profound love FOR them. To choose Christ's dominion and
refuse anyone – no matter how dear – from usurping God's
place, is often to bring Christ into their lives.

Peter left all for Jesus, but the Lord later had a ministry
to Peter's family when the mother-in-law was healed. Then
she rose to serve those who followed Jesus. Also Jesus sent
the disciples out to minister, and then He went to their
own villages to preach. If we radically follow God, He
follows our loved ones.

To choose Jesus often brings Jesus home.

Father, I am jealous for Your place in my life and I am free
by Your dominion. May my family, too, know the joy that is
belonging to You. I trust You with their lives. In Jesus.

DAY 22

Enemies in the House

(Reading Mark 3 in the *Amplified Bible,* Classic) Jesus had just chosen His twelve disciples...

20. Then He went to a house [probably Peter's] but a throng came together again, so that Jesus and His disciples could not even take food.
21. And when those who belonged to Him (His kinsmen) heard it, they went out to take Him by force, for they kept saying, He is out of His mind (beside Himself, deranged)!

Family seeks to control the disciple who is abandoned to follow Christ. Jesus also said – to disciples only – your enemies will be the members of your own household.

Take Christ "by force." Imagine! Of all people, His family knew His true identity, but in the strangeness of His journey and the chaos around Him, they believed it meant He was out of control and out of reality.

"They kept saying, 'He is out of His mind...'" As families do, they talked at length with each other about Him, behind His back, then judged Him and labeled Him. The endless talk escalated until they were the ones irrational and out of reality. The ones who loved Him did not understand Him and became His enemies, even as He was following God and miracles were taking place wherever He went.

It is this kind of control in which families typically think they know the disciple, and naturally feel they have a right to dominate. I believe behind it was the sense that they were losing Him to His disciples, that Peter and the others had become His family...and it was so!

Father, I commit myself fully to the will of God and cast off all restraints from everyone, including myself. I am Yours! Through Jesus.

DAY 23

The One Criterion for Family

Mark 3:31-35 AMPC
Then His mother and His brothers came and, standing outside, they sent word to Him, calling (for) Him. And a crowd was sitting around Him, and they said to Him, Your mother and Your brothers and Your sisters are outside asking for You.

And He replied, Who are My mother and My brothers?

And looking around on those who sat in a circle about Him, He said, See! Here are My mother and My brothers; For whoever does the things God wills is My brother and sister and mother!

It does not appear that Jesus ever went out to meet His family and they certainly never took Him by force.

He seemed simply to ignore their control – even their demand that He leave His gathering and meet them. Jesus did not argue or condemn, but He resolutely did not acquiesce to them in any way. It seems that He just quietly kept His path and His relationships.

But it spoke a very loud NO to the control of His mother, brothers and sisters. Jesus had identified the true family of God and was unmoved in His loyalty to those relationships FIRST.

Jesus was not swayed by demands for family-born loyalties.

The criterion for family is one thing: those who do the will of God! These are disciples who are related to Christ in a bond that God's will reveals. You can be one who meets Christ, but you only enter your union in Him within God's will. Outside God's will is outside Christ's circle of family...

Every believer is born-again into Union with Christ,

but only within God's will is that wonderful Union experienced.

Father, help me to be uncompromisingly committed to Your will. I commit to loyalty over acquiescence. By Jesus.

DAY 24

Jesus' True Family Revealed

JUDE 1, A servant of Jesus Christ (the Messiah) and brother of James (Mark 6:3)
JAMES 1:1, A servant of God and of the Lord Jesus Christ (Mark 6:3)

Jude and James were Jesus' half brothers. They eventually came to see Him as Messiah and bow to His Lordship. They had abandoned their family ties to Him and didn't bother to mention it in their epistles. That natural bond had no eternal meaning. Their relationship to Him was on the basis of being His servant—that is, to serve Him in God's will. Now they were Christ's TRUE FAMILY.

Note from the Amplified Bible: James presided at the Jerusalem council (Acts 15) where the church leaders reached an agreement for the basis of Christian fellowship.

James was a leader in the first century church, but not because of his being the natural brother of Jesus. He came into Christ the same way all others did: receiving Him as Savior within. And he came to live as a servant of his Messiah within God's will. This was the criterion for his leadership.

Jude's writing is an amazing discernment of the nature of false teachers and ways of the wicked. He could only have written this by the Spirit out of a life of severe personal purity from the deepest repentance.

Jesus' family was blessed by His stance of loyalty to God first and His disciples next. Christ had a right view that pain which issues from selfish control that opposes God is illegitimate and un-pitiable. So any pain His family felt because of their rebellion received no sympathy from the

Lord.

But the greatest mystery of this is how did Christ pray for His family so that they came to God? I suppose we will have to learn that in our own lives from the Lord Himself...

Father, hold me so close that I will not be a hindrance to or actually hinder the will of God in my relationships. In Jesus.

DAY 25

A Cross Experience for the Disciple

Continuing with Luke 14:27...

And anyone who does not carry his cross and follow Me cannot be My disciple.

This matter of putting God before our dearest ties is a Cross experience, and that dying is excruciating for both, but precious to God. It is death to relationship, but oneness is the reward.

I don't usually tell a personal story but I want to share this one with you...

My precious daughter has spent time with God to understand my calling, and He has given her valuable insight about His purpose for me. She sees. She has been an amazing supporter to help me walk in my calling, and the Lord has often given her warnings of danger for me.

She went with me to Israel one year and her prayer beforehand was, "Lord, let Mom forget I am here." She purposed to be of no distraction to my responsibilities. I did not know she had been so completely unselfish, and several times during the trip I really did forget she was there. I was horrified at myself but I was free to be focused on the Lord and His agenda.

She had a wonderful time and loved the journey and the people who traveled with us, but she had relinquished having a trip with ME only! She held herself as simply one of the travelers...oh, it was amazing to me. That was a once in a lifetime experience for us, and she was willing to live it only on God's terms.

I was aware she was walking in delight, just alone with

her own Lord and living out her private journey. A dear friend and her husband also made the journey, and they were Julia's travel buddies, so the Lord set it up perfectly for HER as she gave the trip over to Him!

And in that state of surrender, she also formed a relationship that is going to be a blessing in her life and mine. She walked in the Lord's will for her, and so He brought His will TO her. And in addition, she had new insight about my life and discernment about my walk and my needs in traveling.

I have died to her a hundred times and she has died to me. And the Lord has made us one in amazing ways that are very private and wonderful. We are on the same path of God's purpose and will. The Lord loves to make Church out of family, but it happens only through the Cross of dying to self.

Father, I seek oneness in Your will over mere family ties. Unity is the reward of putting You before everyone else, and I want that. Through Jesus.

DAY 26

Spirit of Counsel and Knowledge

Isaiah 11:2 AMPC
And the Spirit of the Lord shall rest upon Him — the Spirit of
wisdom and understanding, the Spirit of counsel and might, the
Spirit of knowledge and of the reverential and obedient fear of the
Lord —

Our human bond to family is a liaison embedded in our soul, so deep and hidden in our very identity that its roots are too complex for our mastery. We do not possess 'wisdom and understanding' of our own selves, much less our family ties!

This calling to 'hate' family is a command, but more, it is an intricate process of the Holy Spirit who alone knows the heart of our loyalties and bondages.

So the Spirit of Christ leads the disciple into the maze of appropriate separation from family. The one who follows the Lamb will hear and know instinctively the Voice of the Savior's jealousy to be First, All, Only. The Father has His own order and perfect timing through His brilliant counsel. It is purely individual, not accomplished in one swift dealing. This one call can take years of dealings at God's instigation.

On my part, it is simple. One small or huge step at a time, as the Lord unveils His will. On the Lord's part, it is a great and complex process in which He leads, reveals and accomplishes until Christ is fully All: my Father, Mother, sister, brother, friend and lover…till every relationship need is placed in Him.

His call is absolute and severe but His patience is astounding. *"He knoweth we are dust."*

Father, search my heart for my loyalties and bondages and set me free. In Jesus.

DAY 27

One Family in Christ Jesus

Galatians 3:26-28 NASB
For you are all sons of God through faith in Christ Jesus. For all
of you who were baptized into Christ have clothed yourselves
with Christ. There is neither Jew nor Greek, there is neither slave
nor free man, there is neither male nor female; for you are all one
in Christ Jesus.

To 'hate' family (Luke 14) is to identify yourself utterly with God as your blood relationship in Christ Jesus. It is a change of your concept of yourself because of the real change in your human standing wrought by Jesus. You are now God's family on this earth!

The most subtle leaving of family, however, is to leave your ethnic identity – the larger family of origin. Francis Frangipane said, "I used to be Italian." It is a profound statement! And rarely made by any Christian. Now there is neither Jew nor Gentile. Neither English nor Australian.

Paul, who was a Jew of Jews, made the above statement to the Galatians. He had left all his Jewish identification and roots, all his Jewish traditions and allowed his knowledge and world to be completely restructured as a son of God. He had one family by having one loyalty, one Father. One Lord!

When our identity is seen as fully in God, only in Christ, then we enjoy amazing oneness with the eternal Body of Christ as true family.

Across every boundary, over every other identification, we are bound and secure as one family.

Father, thank You that my blood relationship is now Christ.
What a family you have given me! Through Jesus.

DAY 28

Belonging to God and His Family

1 Peter 1:18-19 AMPC
You must know (recognize) that you were redeemed (ransomed)
from the useless (fruitless) way of living inherited by tradition
from (your) forefathers, not with corruptible things (such as)
silver and gold,

But [you were purchased] with the precious blood of Christ (the
Messiah), like that of a [sacrificial] lamb without spot or blemish.

Everything in God is seen, not attained. *"It is
finished."* What is? Everything.

My freedom from fallen humanity (my own and my
ancestors) has been accomplished. The enjoyment of that
freedom from human frailty is already mine. I merely agree
to God's demand of His rightful place as Father, Mother —
ALL. I die to family as the Spirit leads. Only then do I see
that it was all accomplished on the Cross.

I WAS severed from human family — it simply waits for me to accept it.

You have been bought and chosen. You are already taken
out of the captivating sins of your human inheritance: the
weakness and shame, the pride and ignorance that resides
in your soul – from the womb.

When I was buried in baptism with Christ, I died to my
identity as sinner, as daughter, as mother. I died with Him
to the old life in EVERY aspect. And I was raised with Him
in resurrection to enjoy belonging to God and His family.
In that divine family, I share His likeness with you and you
display His likeness to me. Yet that's only possible when
we will allow God to bring us to and through this strange
"hate" of family and into His fold as disciples.

This is not some unattainable ideal! It is real...

Father, I can barely take in the enormity of Your gift of salvation, but I praise You that it is finished! By Jesus.

DAY 29

The Heavenly Father Is the Source

Matthew 23:8-9 ESV
But you are not to be called rabbi, for you have one teacher and you are all brothers. And call no man your father on earth, for you have one Father, who is in heaven.

The Heavenly Father is the Source of all Life and all Truth. Humanity, whether born again or not, has the natural propensity to take His place, to tell you what to do, what to say and even who to be. The essence of the call to 'hate father, mother, wife and children, brothers and sisters' is to fiercely 'hate' not just family domination, but anyone who presumes to demand His place who alone is Father.

The disciple is jealous for God as Father, and no human can have that place nor presume that position. The indwelling Life of Jesus is the source of that consuming loyalty and its wisdom to 'hate.'

The Heavenly Father is our ONLY Father.

Father, You created me and I choose to love who YOU made me to be. You are the only Father I need and I belong to You. Through Jesus.

DAY 30

Your Heritage from Family

Luke 14:26 ESV
If anyone comes to Me and does not hate his own father and mother and wife and children and brothers and sisters, yes, and even his own life, he cannot be My disciple.

Your heritage from family is the Adamic nature with all its enmity with God. That nature is incurable. It is destructive at its core and selfish in its motives. Any relationship based on that nature brings an inherent disloyalty to God and a built-in delusion of self-idolatry. It is that nature, that human fallen existence, that Jesus calls us to hate along with the relationships that foster it and call it up from the grave.

Human ties are earthly ties. Human relationships are flesh to flesh. Soul can only meet with soul…and spirit alone can commune with spirit. The absolute severance from every natural human-born relationship, even including with yourself, is really a complete disconnect of FLESH for a life lived solely out of the new spirit by the indwelling Christ.

Father, please help me to know and recognize that I am redeemed from the heritage of my earthly family (1 Peter 1:18). Through Jesus. Thank You for the gift of Your Son!

DAY 31

A Healthy Hatred for My Soul-Life

Luke 14:26 ESV
If anyone comes to Me and does not hate…yes, even his own life,
he cannot be My disciple.

The last great emotional anguish of hatred is to know my true self, and my real motive, under the microscope of God. From the shock of seeing that secret-soul-life comes a healthy hatred.

We will NOT hate our soul-life — we love it, *believe* in it. I must be devastated of its worth by seeing the ravage of my spirit from the delusion of my soul. The soul must become utterly divided from the spirit (Hebrews 4:12). And that is a work of the Spirit by the Word.

To be led of the Spirit, to follow Christ will bring the inevitable unveiling of the soul's identity, then delighted abandonment of living outside of and apart from that hopeless nature.

Father, shine the Light of Christ on my secret-soul-life that I will
be brought to repentance and freed from the delusion of my soul.
By Jesus.

DAY 32

Christ Is My Home

Hebrews 11:13b-16 ESV
...they were strangers and exiles on the earth. For people who speak thus make it clear that they are seeking a homeland. If they had been thinking of that land from which they had gone out, they would have had opportunity to return. But as it is, they desire a better country, that is, a heavenly one. Therefore, God is not ashamed to be called their God, for He has prepared for them a city.

This is discipleship: A saint (very dear to me) recently went to the mission field of her calling. She said, "There was something very strange. I was completely at home there, and when I went back to my house in the states, I was completely at home there, too! I realized that wherever I am is home because...Christ is my home! Christ is my country."

Father, I thank You that wherever I go and whatever happens, in Christ I am home! In Jesus.

DAY 33

Discipleship Is Abandon

Luke 14:26 ESV
If anyone comes to Me and does not hate his own father and
mother and wife and children and brothers and sisters, yes, and
even his own life, he cannot be My disciple.

When Jesus spoke this blank requirement, he was a
guest of a ruler of the Pharisees. In this social setting,
where they are "watching him carefully," He made no
effort to please them, no attempt to appease them.

The Lord made one of His puzzling and shocking
statements, seeming to contradict God's very law. Just in
the place where He could gain some approval, He made
Himself offensive by His radical demands. It was sure to
provoke many to turn away from following Him and give
the Pharisees the very ground to seek His death.

Oswald Chambers wrote: "Jesus Christ is always
unyielding to my claim to my right to myself… The
one essential element in all our Lord's teaching about
discipleship is abandon, no calculation, no trace of self-
interest."

Father, it is no longer I who live but Christ who lives in me, and
I thank You for the privilege of watching Him now live my life
(Galatians 2:20). In Jesus.

DAY 34

The Sword of Love

Matthew 10:34-37 ESV
Do not think that I have come to bring peace to the earth. I have
not come to bring peace, but a sword. For I have come to set a
man against his father, and a daughter against her mother, and
a daughter-in-law against her mother-in-law. And a person's
enemies will be those of his own household. Whoever loves father
or mother more than Me is not worthy of Me, and whoever loves
son or daughter more than Me is not worthy of Me.

These words of Jesus turn to another side of family —
the issue of love. He will Himself bring the sword against
human ties and the test will come at His hand. The test
being: Who do you love? Whose love do you love?

But the real issue revealed here is not our poor human
loves, but the great consuming love of Christ. His is a Love
that loves you entirely and wants your focus, your loyalty,
your whole heart – that you would live and breathe His
love for YOU!

Father, You rejoice over me with gladness, You bring quietness
with Your love, and You delight in me with shouts of joy
(Zephaniah 3:17). May I live and breathe that! In Jesus.

DAY 35

Do You Love Me?

John 21:17 NASB
"Simon, son of John, do you love Me?"

This is the most terrible question possible to the one who has beheld the Son of God and loved Him with passion. This question hangs over us all, and God sees the answer in all our relationships and all situations of relationship. What we love will come out. For all the love Peter felt for Christ, he loved himself the most. Yet Christ knew that by the Holy Spirit, Peter would be infused with such love that he would eventually die for His sake. Jesus trusted Peter with His sheep, because He saw the direction and desire of love, and He knew the coming power of the Spirit was the power TO LOVE HIM.

Peter's love was merely human, great though it was. The Love of God for the Son is "shed abroad in the heart by the Holy Spirit" and it is a love-absolute, a supernatural un-human passion that will carry and propel, enervate and transform!

Father, thank You that You gave us Your Holy Spirit to love You with Your own love and infuse this earthly vessel with passion for Christ. From Jesus.

DAY 36

The Last and Largest Love

Luke 14:26 AMPC
If any man comes to Me and does not hate…[yes] and even his
own life also — he cannot be My disciple.

Oswald Chambers said, "Salvation and discipleship are not the same thing."

The difference between the follower and the disciple is simply love. Humanity was created to adore with absolute passion. It is in our very marrow. But we are capable of corrupting our soul with self-love.

Oswald Chambers' inspired words are always as absolute as is God. About this passage, he wrote this: "Our love for Him must be overwhelmingly more passionate than every devoted relationship."

The last bastion of human passion is the greatest love, the one Jesus mentions last. The one that lies behind every motive and choice. The one that rules me until I come to hate, at last, my infatuation with my soul-self.

Father, I am infatuated with my soul-self. I was created to adore with absolute passion and I commit that to YOU. Through Jesus.

DAY 37

To Love the Lord with Undying Love

Luke 7:37a, 38 NASB
And there was a woman in the city who was a sinner…she
brought an alabaster vial of perfume, and standing behind Him
(Christ) at His feet, weeping, she began to wet His feet with
her tears, and kept wiping them with the hair of her head, and
kissing His feet and anointing them with the perfume.

We don't know who this woman was. The Holy Spirit
deliberately omits her name. But she stands for all those
who love the Lord with undying love. This unknown
woman had a love for Christ that gave Him her time, her
goods, and her heart with abandon. Caring nothing for the
approval of man, the inappropriateness of her action, she
went past this company of arrogant men whose superiority
to her had no longer any power to bring her shame.

She had no need for human approval, understanding,
or respect. Her need? Her goal? To lavish Jesus with the
love she had for Him, a love that produced such humility
and vulnerability that she cared only to express it to Him.
She was indifferent to the scorn of the religious and the
misunderstanding of the watchers. Her great love was the
only care of her soul, the single focus of her heart and all
else was irrelevant and immaterial.

This is a disciple. How does one come to possess or
rather BE possessed of such Love for God?

Father, I desire to be possessed by great Love for You. I choose
to love You with all my heart, with all my soul, and with all my
mind (Matthew 22:37). By Jesus.

DAY 38

Our Gracious and Brilliant Lord

Luke 7:39-43 ESV
Now when the Pharisee who had invited Him saw this, he said
to himself, "If this man were a prophet, He would have known
who and what sort of woman this is who is touching Him, for she
is a sinner." And Jesus answering said to him, "Simon, I have
something to say to you." And he answered, "Say it, Teacher."

"A certain moneylender had two debtors. One owed five hundred
denarii and the other fifty. When they could not pay, he canceled
the debt of both. Now which of them will love him more?"

Simon answered, "The one, I suppose, for whom he canceled the
larger debt." And He said to him, "You have judged rightly."

Jesus is ever both gracious and brilliant. So Simon would
understand and come with Jesus into His explanation
of the woman's passionate deed, He wrapped the issue
inside a story. And then He let Simon draw the obvious
conclusion himself. He entered the man's own world with
the story: the world of commerce and money. How He
knows us! How He comes inside our frame of reference…

Simon had not spoken aloud his proud judgments of
both the Lord and the woman. But Jesus addresses us
by our thoughts and by our heart-values, not by actions
or even words. It is our deep and hidden thinking He
confronts because the heart is the origin of our true
self. Jesus sees all things in direct opposition to human
assessments, and He would transform our thoughts into
His own astonishing views.

Father, search me and know my heart, test me and know my

thoughts, and create in me a pure heart (Psalm 139:23 and Psalm 51:10). Through Jesus.

DAY 39

Passion for Christ

Luke 7:44-46 ESV
Then turning toward the woman He said to Simon, "Do you see this woman? I entered your house; you gave Me no water for My feet, but she has wet My feet with her tears and wiped them with her hair.

You gave Me no kiss, but from the time I came in she has not ceased to kiss My feet.

You did not anoint My head with oil, but she has anointed My feet with ointment."

We can never comprehend love unless we have seen our complete lack of it.

For Simon to understand what he was seeing in this woman, Jesus had to show the man what was NOT in him. Simon had not extended even the basic common courtesies to Jesus as a guest in his house. It had revealed the petty smallness of the man's heart and the contempt he had for the Son of God.

Passion for Christ is ridiculous to those who have not even natural love, whose hearts are void of simple human empathy.

Father, I confess my complete lack of love apart from Jesus. Please give me a passion for Christ as radical as this woman's! By Jesus?

DAY 40

Love in Exact Proportion to Repentance

Speaking to Simon the Pharisee, Jesus said, *"Therefore I tell you, her sins, which are many, are forgiven – for she loved much. But he who is forgiven little, loves little"* (Luke 7:47 ESV).

The whole root of love for Jesus, from which a larger than life passion grows, is simply repentance. Repentance is seeing from God's viewpoint how truly, utterly, totally BAD I am. It is total responsibility without blame or excuse – that alone is repentance that can access forgiveness.

The first message of John the Baptist was "Repent!" The first sermon of Jesus was the call, *"Repent, for the kingdom of God is at hand."*

The size of your love is the size of your forgiven-sin.

The size of your love for Christ is in exact proportion to the size of your repentance.

Father, I desire a huge love for Jesus Christ. Please give me the repentance to match the size of the love I so desire! From Jesus.

DAY 41

Repentance and Transformation

Luke 7:47-48 ESV
"Therefore I tell you, her sins, which are many, are forgiven – for she loved much. But he who is forgiven little, loves little."

And He said to her, "Your sins are forgiven."

Repentance is the door to the kingdom, the way of fruit, the access of divine forgiveness. And the outgrowth is love for the Forgiver.

The religious are exacting of others and blind to their own sin. The thieves and prostitutes go into the kingdom first because they know they are sinners and are closest to repentance.

The word 'repentance' means "to change your mind with abhorrence of your past sins." A root of the Greek word means 'to change your purpose.'

Repentance is SEEING from God's perspective what you do not see from yours… It changes your thinking, and then your values. Above all, it directs you to a different goal and meaning for your life. So from the inside to the outside, your being and your course are forever changed.

True repentance is real transformation.

Father, open the eyes of my heart that I might see and repent deeply and be transformed utterly. Through Jesus.

DAY 42

Love Alone Embraces the Cross

Luke 14:27 AMPC
Whoever does not persevere and carry his own cross and come after (follow) Me cannot be My disciple.

The difference between a believer and a disciple is LOVE.

Love is only love which MUST follow the Beloved no matter where He leads, even to the loss of life and self and choice and rights. Love alone embraces the Cross.

Father, I embrace the work of the Holy Spirit that I may follow You wherever You lead and whatever the cost. For Jesus.

DAY 43

The Brilliance of the Word

Luke 14:27 NASB
Whoever does not carry his own cross and come after Me cannot be My disciple.

The Bible is so brilliant that it takes the mind and counsel of God to break open the treasure. The sections flow from one jeweled Truth to another, each one picturing the last and amplifying the whole. Scripture explains scripture in the most wonderful way. May the Father give us eyes and ears for His Word!

Luke 14 is a complete picture of discipleship, and this verse is the core topic of the whole. Discipleship is determined by the acceptance of the Cross. And the woman is a real story of disciple abandonment and her secret is love-from-forgiveness.

Of what the woman who washed Jesus' feet repented, we are not told. Her repentance and God's forgiveness have erased all of it forever. But Luke 15 – the parable of the prodigal – is the most vivid picture of repentance, setting forth the process, the sequence and the result!

(Since I deal verse by verse and topic by topic, my spirit just wanted to stop and look with awe at the bigger picture: the marvel of His Bible!)

Father, please impart to me the LIFE contained in Luke 14 and 15, giving me eyes and ears for Your precious Word. Through Jesus.

DAY 44

The Cross Is a Divide

Luke 14:27 AMPC
Whosoever does not persevere and carry his own cross and come after (follow) Me cannot be My disciple.

The Cross is the situation or relationship that you cannot control, cannot escape and do not want. It cuts across your will, confronts your strength and attacks your dream. The Cross 'crosses you up.' It cuts across your path and ever makes a new fork in your road. The Cross is ever a choice, a pivot of your history.

The Cross is the pivot of human history, the marker of eras, the end of human misery. It is the great mystery of God and only those who carry their own Cross – their personal dying for Jesus' sake – know its secrets.

The Cross is the great divide between believer and disciple. The disciple is proven by the Cross. The believer is exposed by the unwillingness to die.

Father, reveal my Cross to me today. I commit to this Cross. For Jesus.

DAY 45

The Cross Is Love

Matthew 10:38 NASB
And he who does not take his cross and follow after Me is not worthy of Me.

The Cross is ever presented as a choice. YOU take it up. YOU carry it. YOU deny yourself.

No 'deep teaching' can take you to a Cross life. No brilliant explanation will cause you to give your all for Jesus. No human appeal will ever be enough. The Holy Spirit must take you there by a unique process of His knowledge of YOU. And the way He takes is for Love, by Love through the loss of every other love. The Cross is a love sacrifice, a love answer to Jesus and only that.

The disciple is one who has repented and seen Him, loved Him, and died *for Him.*

And…*"few there be that find it."*

Father, take me, lead me to my Cross. I truly want to be one of the "few" who find it. With Jesus.

DAY 46

The Power of God

1 Corinthians 1:18 AMPC
For the story and message of the cross is sheer absurdity and folly
to those who are perishing and on their way to perdition but to
us who are being saved it is the (manifestation of) the power of
God.

The power of the Cross is that all was solved there and
it is the perfect (but ONLY) solution to humanity's total
depravity. The Cross has the power to transform you…
there is NO other place of such power.

The Cross will set you free of your Adamic self. It is
your dearest friend, your piercing examiner! The Cross
comes to the very core of your idolatry and the unseen
place of your independence. Idolatry and independence:
the two deadly aspects of human nature from Eden.

Your personal Cross will take you out of the prison of
self and make you what you never were and never could
be. All because of Christ's life poured out and given – TO
YOU. Through the Cross Jesus is resurrected and released
within you and lives AS you!

The Cross is the end of you AND the beginning of you.

Father, thank You for freeing me from the prison of self. I
welcome the end of me that the Cross brings and rejoice in my
new creation. Thank You for this glorious gift! Through Jesus.

DAY 47

The Cross Is the Zeal of God

Romans 6:4-5 ESV
We were buried therefore with Him by baptism into death, in order that, just as Christ was raised from the dead by the glory of the Father, we too might walk in newness of life.

For if we have been united with Him in a death like His, we shall certainly be united with Him in a resurrection like His.

The Cross of Christ is eternal and unending. It is so dynamic that is has never ceased its power or presence. Yet for me the Cross has two aspects and two points in time: Then and Now.

That I am dead to self is a fact, historical and actual. I can count on that fact as faith to live. I may walk through all difficult times and all simple living as one who is removed and gone: "reckon yourself dead to sin."

The Cross is also a current-present-ongoing encounter with God's knowledge of me. The Cross finds the pockets of my old self and the zeal of God brings pressure to end the Adamic nature that the Second Adam may rise anew.

Father, the work of the Cross is fact, then and now. I am dead to sin and dead to self and I will BELIEVE. In Jesus.

DAY 48

The Cross Began in Gethsemane

Matthew 26:39 AMPC
And going a little farther, He threw Himself upon the ground on His face and prayed saying, My Father, if it is possible, let this cup pass away from Me; nevertheless, not what I will [not what I desire], but as You will and desire.

What a painful agony our Lord suffered! *"My soul is sorrowful even to death..."* What a poignant cry! *"My Father, if it be possible, let this cup pass from Me, nevertheless, not as I will but as You will."*

In this rare glimpse at Gethsemane, we are ushered right into Jesus' secret dealings with His Father! We are not told what His travail was about. Speculation abounds, but the scripture gives us the bare essence, the 'bottom line.' And it is enough... This great heaving was the surrender of His will to the Father's will.

And that is death to the soul.

Father, I thank You for Christ's perfect example of surrender. I, too, commit my life and will to Yours. By Jesus.

DAY 49

The Cross and the Will

Matthew 26:39 ESV
And going a little farther He fell on His face and prayed,
saying, "My Father, if it be possible, let this cup pass from Me;
nevertheless, not as I will, but as You will."

The death of the soul is the surrender of the will. The will is the lead of the whole life. What you *will* to do, you do! Where you *will* to go, you go. The heart is the core of life but the will is the leader that rises out of the heart to pursue its direction. To give your will over to God is to die in surrender.

Jesus knew well the cup He would drink on the Cross. It was the cup of the wrath of God for all the sin of humanity (Isaiah 51:17). And it meant total separation from God.

No one but Christ could drink that cup, but in our surrender, we will taste the death of the soul when we are asked to go a way that is against our strong desire.

Father, to follow Jesus, I must deny my self. It is a choice to surrender the will, and I choose to surrender mine to Yours. In Jesus.

DAY 50

The Cross: Abandon Self for God

Luke 9:23 AMPC (Emphasis Mine)
And He said to all, If any person wills to come after Me, let him deny himself [disown himself, forget, lose sight of himself and his own interests, refuse and give up himself] and take up his cross daily and follow Me [cleave steadfastly to Me, conform wholly to My example in living and, if need be, in dying also].

The *Amplified Bible* gives the most profound definition of what it means to deny yourself. And this version describes perfectly the manner of "following" – to cleave, conform, and die.

There are four great words that surround the Cross.

- **IF**: the choice. The Cross and discipleship are the same issue, but they are always a free choice.

- **WILLS**: the surrender of the will.

- **COME AFTER ME**: Follow Christ – not thrills, not perks, not causes, not people, but the Lord Jesus.

- **DENY**: reject, renounce, forgo your Self's dreams, ambition, desires, and above all, *rights*. Abandon self for HIM.

The Cross is ever a choice, daily a choice to take God's side against your own self-preservation and self-exaltation.

Father, for all the many Crosses I will face, I commit to embrace them as Your will and choice for my life. In Jesus.

DAY 51

You Boast About What You Love

Galatians 6:14-16 NIV
May I never boast except in the cross of our Lord Jesus Christ,
through which the world has been crucified to me and I to
the world. Neither circumcision nor uncircumcision means
anything; what counts is a new creation. Peace and mercy to all
who follow this rule, even to the Israel of God.

You boast about what you love, you point to what helps
you, you brag about what sets you free. The Jews boasted
in circumcision. Paul boasted in the Cross. Christ on the
Cross was his liberty from himself and the entrance into
the new creation. Peace and mercy were the result of the
Cross embraced.

Peace and mercy! What we so need from God, lavishly
given by and through the Cross. Paul came to know the
two aspects of the Cross:

- What Christ gained and gave us at Calvary, and

- The power of the Cross in its current dynamic to
  bring forth the new creation that Christ bought.

Father, for the lavish gift of the Cross, I praise You! Jesus is my
liberty and my LIFE. From Jesus.

DAY 52

Crucified to the World

Galatians 6:14 ESV
But far be it from me to boast except in the cross of our Lord
Jesus Christ, by which the world has been crucified to me, and I
to the world.

When the Cross becomes a lifestyle – a way of receiving God in life – it operates as a great force, a power that strikes your soul and kills what will not die. The Cross is a literal blow that lays you low for three days or more and then resurrection life rises and you enter the new creation without the old one tugging at you. Whatever area was struck is unable to rise again—it is truly dead.

Not only is the old nature dead but the susceptibility to the pull of this world is crucified also: ambition, lusts, loves, greed, need for approval…

Father, thank You for the Cross of Jesus Christ that crucifies the world to me and me to the world! Through Jesus.

DAY 53

The Cost of the Call

Reading Luke 14:28-32 NASB
28. For which one of you, when he wants to build a tower, does not first sit down and calculate the cost to see if he has enough to complete it?

31. Or what king, when he sets out to meet another king in battle, will not first sit down and consider whether he is strong enough with ten thousand men to encounter the one coming against him with twenty thousand?

The Lord Jesus Christ is so perfect in integrity that He gives you always the cost of the call. There are two aspects to discipleship: building and fighting. You see it in Nehemiah. You see it in Paul. He was ever both building the church and fighting the enemy.

Luke records Jesus' warning of the cost of the call. Not so much 'count the cost' and then decide, but KNOW the cost: it is and will be…everything! Discipleship will cost you everything you are and all that you possess.

1. You will spend all to build God's will on earth for your destiny.

2. It will be war against an enemy stronger (twice as many) than you with whom you may not compromise nor ever 'make peace.'

The secret is this: it is what you were created to do. It is your great (and only) adventure in this life…to build God's will on earth and to defeat His enemy in battle. It requires everything of you, but the other secret is that everything is supplied to you in Christ!

Oh, what a small price is discipleship compared with the exceeding great reward of knowing HIM.

Father, help me to count the cost, reveal to me my cost of discipleship. In Jesus.

DAY 54

The Cost of Building and Battling

Reading Luke 14:28-33 NASB (Emphasis Mine)
For which one of you when he wants to build a tower, does not first sit down and calculate the cost…?

Or what king, when he sets out to meet another king in battle, will not first sit down and consider whether he is strong enough…?

So then, none of you can be My disciple who does not give up all his own possessions.

The Lord Jesus presents the calling of the disciple: building and battling. No need to consider the cost because you cannot anticipate the adventure to which you are committing. It is a blank contract. You choose to sign on as a disciple and the Lord fills in the conditions as you go. All the way through, it is YOUR choice.

In all integrity, Jesus Himself gives you the cost of building and battling: everything you are and everything you have. The cost is total. And you will only finish the building and you will only win the battle if you give ALL.

For the builder…your possessions, your self.
For the warrior…your existence, your body.

The cost is everything.

Father, I choose to sign Your blank contract for me. I choose to sign on as Your disciple. Through Jesus.

DAY 55

A Terrifyingly Beautiful Process

A note from Helen, one who knows the Cross: "Over the years, and especially in recent years, I have realized that the Holy One has been so kind and careful, making His claim on that "all" gradually. Or perhaps it's better to say that He has deepened that claim beyond things and moved to actions, hopes, beliefs, even to the very core of me.

"And with each deepening of His claim, my dependence on Him has become more complete and desperate. A terrifyingly beautiful process."

Father, I surrender all and I love You. In Jesus.

DAY 56

The End of Effort

Luke 14:33 NASB
*So then none of you can be My disciple who does not give up all
his own possessions.*

Down under the obvious possessions is possessiveness
– the base tendency of our nature. The first 'possession'
is EFFORT. It is the independent thinking of "I can do it
without God." Jesus refused ever to use human effort to
achieve God's will.

The temptations of Jesus were to these very Adamic
qualities. Satan essentially said, "Use the effort of the flesh
to turn stones into bread." It is to these 'powers' we must
die by letting go, making an end of effort.

Jesus explained His miracles by saying, *"I assure you,
most solemnly I tell you, the Son is able to do nothing of Himself
(of His own accord)…* (John 5:19 AMPC).

Jesus considered the effort of the flesh to amount to
'nothing.' His effort, energy, and achievement came from
the Life of the Father within Him. He simply would not
exert the power of the flesh, that human power which
CAN produce great things that end only in disaster.

To meet your own needs, living by your Adamic
strength without leaning entirely on God—this is the
ability and effort of the old self. And the Cross exposes the
futility of our effort and offers an end to the nature that
believes it doesn't need God.

Behind our human actions and our independence of
God is the simple issue of effort…and it must die!

Father, I commit to the power of Your Life to accomplish, I surrender my will to Yours, and I abandon my human effort. By Jesus.

DAY 57

The Cross and the Nature of Man

Luke 14:33 NASB
So then none of you can be My disciple who does not give up all his own possessions.

We think of possessions as objects, jobs, family, or material things. But God sees ownership by its motive. He sees possession as the issue of what you would CONTROL.

The three temptations of Jesus reveal the Adamic nature as God sees it. The first temptation was to exert Adamic flesh-effort (turn stones into bread). Control matter for your own self.

The next temptations were about control or…it could be said another way: lust for power. 'Jump off the tower and force God to catch you.' Control of God. The very base nature of man wants to control God, and the wise discover He will not be controlled and cannot be manipulated.

The third temptation was to rule people. There Satan revealed his underlying agenda: to worship himself instead of God.

To exert force and control over others is to worship Satan, and to worship Satan is to be controlled by Satan.

So the death of self is the relinquishment of EFFORT and CONTROL. These make up the core nature of the old self. This is the very NATURE of humanity that must die by the workings of the Cross through life experiences.

Father, I relinquish my effort and control over matter, man, and YOU. I embrace the Crosses You send to make it so! In Jesus.

DAY 58

The Disciple and the Kingdom

Luke 14:33 NASB
So then none of you can be My disciple who does not give up all
his own possessions.

Jesus' prayer of John 17:10 – *"All things that are Mine are Yours, and Yours are Mine…"*

The whole conflict (human and satanic) of the world is for ownership…not just rulership, but actual ownership. The disciple takes God's side that He owns all by relinquishing the rights of ownership—of people, things, positions and places.

This is the Cross: to divest yourself of ownership.

Then the wonder is this: when God owns ALL, then ALL He owns is ALL yours.

"Blessed are the poor in spirit for theirs is the kingdom of heaven." The 'poor' is one who owns/possesses nothing. The kingdom has everything and only the poor (beggarly) in spirit enjoy its citizenship. Most want the kingdom without the deep personal poverty that is its condition. It does not say that the poor ENTER the kingdom; it says *"theirs is the kingdom of heaven."* All the glory and riches of the kingdom belongs to the one who will "give up all his possessions."

This is simply following the Lord Jesus.

Father, show me all the things in my life that I hold and own and grip. Show me all the things that possess me. Through Jesus.

DAY 59

Raised by the Power of Resurrection

Ephesians 1:18-20a NASB
I pray that the eyes of your heart may be enlightened, so that you
will know what is the hope of His calling, what are the riches
of the glory of His inheritance in the saints, and what is the
surpassing greatness of His power toward us who believe. These
are in accordance with the working of the strength of His might,
which He brought about in Christ, when He raised Him from the
dead...

The other side of the Cross is a whole new life, the very
Life of Christ by the POWER of resurrection. Sometimes
you can experience the change, but most of the time you
are not aware of how great a transformation has taken you
over.

Resurrection is a very great and wonderful mystery.
Through the Cross, the very Life of Christ rises in you.
Where you died, He lives. Where you relinquished, He
took over. His holy nature replaces your unholy nature.

We are meant to live on the resurrection side, where
Christ the Lord is the entire explanation of a wondrous life.

He thinks, He endures, He conquers, He speaks...
instead of me. Jesus is the 'Person' I cannot be. He is the
power I do not have. Above all, He loves where I cannot
and is then the One-Love of my life.

Father, I long for the resurrection side of the Cross, where I am
dead and You live. And where I have relinquished and You have
taken over. In Jesus.

DAY 60

Enemies of the Cross

Philippians 3:18 NASB
For many walk, of whom I often told you, and now tell you even
weeping, that they are enemies of the cross of Christ...

Watchman Nee wrote that you can be a friend of Jesus but an enemy of the Cross.

It is possible to survive the Cross without dying when it comes. "Many," said Paul (and he is speaking to the Church), fortress their hearts against suffering and will not relinquish rights or control. They are enemies of the Cross.

Some are able to surrender with a measured bowing, but at the core of it, refuse to die to Self. Some, by sheer human endurance, just refuse to be conquered. These emerge with false spirituality, secret bitterness and hardened hearts. I have seen believers go through the most terrible experiences and never die into letting Christ become actual King of all.

The Cross is the dividing line between believer and disciple. The Cross is the bond of fellowship...or the obstacle to Body life.

Father, I relinquish my rights and control. I open my heart to receive from You every Cross I need to be Your disciple. Through Jesus.

DAY 61

Disciples Are Builders

Luke 14:27 NASB
Whoever does not carry his own cross and come after Me cannot be My disciple.

28. ...he wants to build a tower
30. ...this man began to build

I am so excited to come back to the two activities of disciples: building and fighting. Disciples are impelled to build – *"he wants to build."*

Through Love and the Cross, disciples are transformed into builders. Disciples are builders! And the building is...the Church. Not *A* church, but *THE* Church—that wonderful, transcendent connection of born-again ones that Christ Himself links into a Body of His design. One here, several there, some meeting together—this is Church. Church is formed by Christ's Love and connected by the mysterious design of God.

But KNOW THIS, dear readers! Disciples don't build a ministry for themselves, for their ambitions. The saints are not to be used to build a ministry FOR a leader. The disciples build the saints INTO a ministry to the Lord. By the Spirit, disciples build saints into...Church!

The Lord builds His own Church; no human can build what is Christ's Church. But disciples are instruments of His passion, tools of His chiseling, laborers of His fittings... They are vessels of His heart and listeners to His praying.

Father, I confess my personal ambition and building for self. Please make me a builder of Church, the Body of Christ. By Jesus.

DAY 62

Ministry to the Church

Paul's idea of ministry differs radically from ours today.

He was writing to compare the glory of the Law on the face of Moses with the glory of the present age of the Church. And he described his own purpose to the Corinthians and to all the churches.

2 Corinthians 3:8-9 AMPC (Emphasis Mine)
Why should not the dispensation of the Spirit **[this spiritual ministry whose task it is to cause men to obtain and be governed by the Holy Spirit]** *be attended with much greater and more splendid glory?*

For if the service that condemns [the ministration of doom] had glory how infinitely more abounding in splendor and glory must be the service that makes righteous **[the ministry that produces and fosters righteous living and right standing with God]***!*

Do you see? How wonderful! Real ministry is to *'cause men to obtain and be governed by the Holy Spirit,'* to bring God's children to right relationship with God. That is building! That is Church building, one by one. And that alone is ministry. Oh, it does have greater glory!

But that building, that ministry to the church will break your heart, cost your life, and bring down on you terrible persecution, misunderstanding and loss of reputation. That building-ministry will itself be your own deep, continuing Cross, killing everything that is not solely for and by the Lord. It was so for Paul. But, praise God, a few become willing to *'be governed by the Holy Spirit'* and they will be the joy of your heart and the glory of Jesus.

*Father, I purpose to obtain and be governed by the Holy Spirit. I
desire to be in right standing with You above all else. In Jesus.*

DAY 63

Supreme Head of the Church

> *Ephesians 1:22-23 AMPC (Emphasis Mine)*
> *And He has put all things under His feet and has appointed*
> *Him **the universal and supreme Head of the church** [a*
> *headship exercised throughout the church], which is His body,*
> *the fullness of Him Who fills all in all [for in that body lives the*
> *full measure of Him Who makes everything complete and Who*
> *fills everything everywhere with Himself].*

When you were born again, you were born INTO Christ's Body. You are a member, a vital part of THE Church, the heavenly order that is truly Church.

Your enjoyment of the fullness of Christ, your participation in Church, is dependent on His actual Lordship in your deepest walk of life. And that was Paul's work, to call saints over and over back into and under the Lordship of Christ. This is ministry! And this alone is Church: "To be governed by the Holy Spirit."

Church IS and happens where Christ is Lord. 'Church' doesn't have to be pumped up, shouted about, advertised. Just help people surrender to the Lordship of Christ and Church will appear. It has nothing to do with meetings, organizations, or projects. It has to do ONLY with Christ as Lord. Jesus as Lord, Master, King—not in talk, not in sloppy sentimentality, not in grandiosity. *Lord...*

Father, I submit to Jesus Christ as my Lord. Please bring me to
know Him that way in all reality. Through Jesus.

DAY 64

The Boss: Jesus Christ, the Head

Luke 2:25, 26 NASB
Simeon…was righteous and devout, looking for the consolation
of Israel; and the Holy Spirit was upon him.

And it had been revealed to him by the Holy Spirit that he would
not see death before he had seen the Lord's Christ (or Messiah).

Church is to be the manifestation of Christ on this earth
– Jesus appearing through a people! And that only happens
when He is the Source, the Life, and above all…the HEAD
of each individual.

Once, I was moving my father's estate. My dear friend
Jack, the moving man, picked up a picture of Simeon
holding the baby Jesus and gazing at Him. Jack looked
at that picture very carefully and this huge man, with
such loving softness (as if only to himself), said, "Ah, the
Boss…"

Now I tell you, few even know that Christ is to be
literally the Boss, much less *love* the fact that HE IS!

Father, I commit to Jesus as my Source, my Life, and my true
Head. You are the Boss! For Jesus.

DAY 65

Church Is Christ

Ephesians 2:21 AMPC
In Him the whole structure is joined (bound, welded) together
harmoniously, and it continues to rise (grow, increase) into a
holy temple in the Lord [a sanctuary dedicated, consecrated and
sacred to the presence of the Lord].

The disciple who lives a life of the Cross is being built into the Church.

There is a building going on, a hidden structure that only one who dies for Him can see. Oh, if we could only see this Holy Building and the purpose for it. Church is free of human ambitions and meaningless agendas!

If we could savor and pray over every word of this verse, an amazement would rise in us! *"In Him..."* Church exists by, through and in Christ. IN Him, we are Church.

CHURCH IS CHRIST!

Father, You are the Head of my life, the Head of the Church, and
I am found only IN Jesus. Through Jesus.

DAY 66

A Holy Temple

Ephesians 2:21 AMPC
In Him the whole structure is joined (bound, welded) together
harmoniously, and it continues to rise (grow, increase) into a
holy temple in the Lord [a sanctuary dedicated, consecrated and
sacred to the presence of the Lord].

"*Structure...*" Church is a vast organization that exists
in Christ, transcending denomination, time, and distance.
He is building, gathering the ones who abide in Him
from *every place,* by a joining that is filled with harmony,
not discord. Commitment, not division. Holiness, not
commonness.

"*A holy temple in the Lord...*" The temple now is the
people who exist for Christ. Church is for the focus and
presence of Christ! It is "*dedicated, consecrated and sacred*
*to the **presence of the Lord.**"*

Father, You have made me a holy temple. "Lord, I believe, help
thou mine unbelief!" Through Jesus.

DAY 67

An Abode for God

Ephesians 2:21b-22 AMPC
...a holy temple in the Lord [a sanctuary dedicated, consecrated
and sacred to the presence of the Lord]. In Him [and in fellowship
with one another] you yourselves also are being built up [into
this structure] with the rest, to form a fixed abode (dwelling
place) of God in (by, through) the Spirit.

Church is built by God through the Spirit, and we are being formed to fit together as an abode for Christ, an expression of Christ. That is Church: Christ living and being.

God is specific to His Master Plan and uncompromising as to His ultimate intentions – Christ Jesus as Church, because Church IS Christ.

He will not change to our blueprint. God will let you have your own building if you must, but He will not sustain what He does not ordain, nor indwell what He did not build.

Just as He gave the plan to Moses for the tabernacle and to Solomon for the temple, He is orchestrating, with meticulous care, each saint's preparation to be a living stone, fitted for His Home.

Father, thank You for forming me into a home for the expression
of Jesus Christ! By Jesus.

DAY 68

The Presence of the Lord

> *Ephesians 2:21b AMPC (Emphasis Mine)*
> *...a holy temple in the Lord [a sanctuary dedicated, consecrated and sacred to **the presence of the Lord**].*

Church is to be a place where the actual presence of the Lord is evident—His words, His Life, His gifts. Each one is to bring the presence of the Lord. And His presence only accompanies His Lordship.

There are two problems with church today. One is that the presence of the Lord is utterly missing from church meetings. But the second is probably more dangerous. It is the soulish counterfeit that purports to be His presence but is actually the pompous activity of flesh, pretending to be spiritual.

The Cross eliminates the soul, so to avoid the Cross is to remain tragically soulish. And the damage of soulish activity is to prevent the Church from manifesting the real presence of Christ.

T. Austin-Sparks writes: "You can have everything that is in the New Testament counterfeited in the realm of the soul, the psychical. The people who dwell in the realm of their souls become a complete contradiction to what true life in the spirit is, and oh, what havoc the devil has made; what confusion, what chaos and what dishonor to the Lord along that line!"

Father, I commit to You because YOU are what I want, not the counterfeit. For Jesus.

DAY 69

Where Jesus Is Lord, People Are Church

Jesus declared that where *"two or three are gathered IN MY NAME I am there in their midst"* (Matthew 18:20 NASB).

One is an individual in relationship with his or her Savior. That is foundational. But two or three together, meeting around their Lord—this is Church. People are Church, but the issue is not simply that two or three are meeting. The sole issue is whether they are meeting in His name. That is, in His Life, His Lordship, His Headship...all from surrender to Him. *This is Church!*

Believers can enjoy church life in all places, at any time. Church is Christ's Headship! And that doesn't negate any organization or denomination. It doesn't condemn a church building. The issue is Life. Christ's Life is Church. Where He is Lord, with two or more, there is the wonder of His life.

Father, I want to experience You as Head. I want to live as Church for the glory of Your Kingdom. Through Jesus.

DAY 70

God's Consecrated People

Ephesians 4:12 AMPC
His (Father's) intention was the perfecting and the full
equipping of the saints (His consecrated people), [that they
should do] the work of ministering toward building up Christ's
body (the church)...

Disciples are builders. And builders train other builders
for the Building: the Church. But disciples can build
only *"consecrated people."* Consecration means simply those
who are 'set apart' for God alone, owned by and possessed
by God. It is those who are willing to die for the One they
love.

Cross-people can be built into builders.

So before there can be true building of believers, there
has to be a patient suffering – often very long term – to
nurture and call them to enter complete consecration
(belonging, surrendered and under the government of the
Son). *"HIS consecrated people."*

Once you are truly HIS, Christ's Body functions in a
flow of natural unity. Amazing harmony without the effort
to produce it!

Father, You have a consecrated people and I would be one of them
in every way. By Jesus.

DAY 71

The Cost of the Conflict

There are volumes that could be written about discipleship. The Lord seems to be focused this morning on warfare. Let's go back to the scripture we have been addressing on the cost of the conflict.

Luke 14:31-33 AMPC
Or what king going out to engage in conflict with another king, will not first sit down and consider and take counsel whether he is able with ten thousand [men] to meet him who comes against him with twenty thousand?

And if he cannot [do so], when the other king is still a great way off, he sends an envoy and asks the terms of peace.

So then, any of you who does not forsake (renounce, surrender claim to, give up, say good-bye to) all that he has cannot be My disciple.

The first parable of discipleship is about the building of the Church. Warfare is against that investment in Christ's Body.

Satan wants the centrality and the worship that belongs to our Lord Jesus, so his most vicious attack will be in the place and in the lives of disciples who are devoted to the Church.

Slander, discouragement, misunderstanding, accusation, criticism, division—these are some of the diabolical plans of the enemy to discredit disciples and destroy the building of saints into union, a structure which can manifest Christ.

Paul's suffering included actual physical sufferings: beatings, sickness, near drownings. He was often blocked by Satan and said so. He was persecuted, hounded, imprisoned.

Paul seldom described the conflicts of his warfare, but when he did, he wrote in *triumph*.

Father, I thank You that no matter what I suffer or what Satan sends my way, YOU are triumphant always. In Jesus.

DAY 72

Victory in the Vessel

2 Corinthians 4:7-10 NASB
But we have this treasure in earthen vessels, so that the surpassing greatness of the power will be of God and not from ourselves; we are afflicted in every way, but not crushed; perplexed, but not despairing; persecuted, but not forsaken; struck down, but not destroyed; always carrying about in the body the dying of Jesus, so that the life of Jesus also may be manifested in our body.

I have learned a lot about our Lord Jesus from observing Paul. Not Paul's words alone but his attitude, his resilience and, most amazing, his unassailable joy. The explanation of Paul's phenomenal energy and supernatural enthusiasm is…Christ's life.

Jesus, the Son of God, is the treasure in the earthen vessel.

His victory within Paul rose to triumph over every assault because He defeated and disarmed the enemy on the Cross. Not only does Christ live within the disciple, the victory of Christ resides within as well. Jesus is the victory in the vessel. His victory is so complete, so perfect, that nothing of this warfare can ultimately defeat you so long as you rely on Him.

Father, You defeated and disarmed the enemy on the Cross, and now Jesus is the victory in my life! From Jesus.

DAY 73

Jesus' Prayer in Warfare

Luke 22:31 NASB
Simon, Simon, behold, Satan has demanded permission to sift
you like wheat; but I have prayed for you, that your faith may
not fail...

Jesus' prayers were bare and to the marrow of the need.

This is our great model for prayer in warfare. The issue is not despair, failure, fear, intimidation...the issue is FAITH. The assault is not *about* me or *against* me, but against my FAITH in the Father and the Son. When my faith is gone, I am gone.

This is the complete exposure of how the enemy attacks. Peter's problem *seemed* to be fear, but behind it was Satan. Peter's problem *appeared* to be disloyalty, but the real problem was that his faith in Christ as Son of God was shaken. Character failures are faith failures. When things seemed awry, Peter lost what he had heard from the Savior.

The war against the saints and the Church is to ***get us into SELF***, into feelings and self-consciousness, into reasoning. The intent is to remove our gaze from the Lord and His sufficiency, to distract us from listening to His voice.

Father, help me to understand that the enemy's assault is not about me or against me, but against my faith in YOU. I abandon self and look to You! Through Jesus.

DAY 74

We Will Be Sifted Like Wheat

Luke 22:31-32 NASB
Simon, Simon, behold, Satan has demanded permission to sift
you like wheat; but I have prayed for you, that your faith may
not fail; and you, when once you have turned again, strengthen
your brothers.

Sifted like wheat. Wheat was tossed into the air and the chaff was blown off the kernel of wheat. God allows the enemy to remove the chaff. Chaff is that crusty shell that hides the life of God under the bushel of SELF.

Personal warfare is the crisis that exposes how much self is left, and warfare is one thing for Satan, another from God's view. You decide who wins. Paul used his suffering to die and die and obtain the LIFE of wheat and not chaff. Once God has the bare wheat it can be ground and turned into bread that could be served to others. This is what Jesus meant when He said that once you are converted, minister to your brothers. Out of your warfare and from your victory, you become a vessel of Bread to feed the Church with the Life of Christ.

Father, I choose for the warfare in my life to serve YOUR
purpose, not the enemy's. I would be a vessel of Your Bread and
not the enemy's chaff. In Jesus.

DAY 75

Soldier of Christ Jesus

2 Timothy 2:3-4 AMPC
Take (with me) your share of the hardships and suffering
[which you are called to endure] as a good (first-class) soldier of
Christ Jesus. No soldier when in service gets entangled in the
enterprises of [civilian] life; his aim is to satisfy and please the
one who enlisted him.

The schemes of Satan make the world look chaotic and complex to the extreme. Situations and people reach out to entangle you in a human spider web when the REAL combat is with principalities and powers of the air.

In warfare, you first have to hear the Commander. His voice and guidance strip the bizarre down to the simple. There is a Commander you are under, One who oversees the conflict, who knows the issues – the real issues – not the smoke or swirl.

Warfare is training to rule and reign with Christ, so its issues have to do with eternal outcomes. Learning to rule is actually learning to hear, training to *represent* the Commander, not to *command* the Commander or take on the enemy. This is a peculiar warfare and you are in training to fight it the right way. Much of our approach to warfare is finding out, "This is not the way!"

Father, You are my Commander-in-Chief and I, as Your soldier,
will follow. Through Jesus.

DAY 76

Faith and Surrender Were the Victory

Reading Matthew 4, *The Temptation of Jesus:*

Then Jesus was led up by the Spirit into the wilderness to be tempted by the devil.

But He answered and said, "It is written, 'Man shall not live on bread alone, but on every word that proceeds out of the mouth of God.'"
(Verses 1 and 4, NASB)

Jesus defeated Satan by His faith in the Word of God. His faith came from His surrender to the Voice of God out of the Word of God. He was not using Scripture as a magic sword. It was the precept of God from the Voice of God, and He answered with His own surrender from His oneness with God. He would not be separated from His Father.

Jesus' sword was the Word to which He had bowed. His faith and surrender to God were the victory. Not fighting, not striving, but rather His simple allegiance to WHO God is.

Paul said we are more than conquerors through HIM… It was about the Person of God that Jesus answered His tempter.

And the devil departed, defeated.

Father, do I take the Word You give me and work to believe it with all my being? Have I made Your Word my sword? By Jesus.

DAY 77

Priests and Disciples

Luke 14:33 NASB
So then, none of you can be My disciple who does not give up all his own possessions.

The priests of the Old Testament could own nothing, yet the best was theirs. They could own no land, but land was allotted to them. Others could own. Priests could not. The Lord Himself was their inheritance.

In the Old Testament, priests were born to the office and had no choice but to live under the law of the priesthood. Believers of the New Testament are offered discipleship as a choice. Yet it is still a 'born again' matter. When you are born again in Christ, you are destined for discipleship and priesthood.

All believers can come into the priesthood. All believers are called to be priests of the New Covenant, which is to say, disciples of the Lord Jesus. It seems from the Lord's own words that one of the great conditions of discipleship – the IF and the pivot – is to "give up all his own possessions."

Father, as Your disciple, I am owned and possessed by You. And ONLY You. Please make it so! Through Jesus.

DAY 78

The Heart's Possessions

Luke 14:33 NASB
So then, none of you can be My disciple who does not give up all
his own possessions.

The Lord is ever concerned with the heart, only the heart. All of life is the exposure of the heart.

The calling is not necessarily to give away all you have. It is the heart's sense of possessiveness. It is the heart, the secret loves of the heart, that the Lord is going to probe. What you 'own' – possess and treasure – owns you by your own heart's affection.

Watchman Nee writes that we are to give the Lord ownership of everything without reservation. What He gives back and allows us to keep is then 'sanctified,' and that simply means it belongs to the Lord.

What you own, you love. And what you own, owns you.

The Lord demands all the heart by requiring all the possessions of the heart. The disciple is one who has given the entire heart to the Lord—all affections, all masters… all possessions. And from the disciple, the Lord may take away whatever He pleases at any time.

The Lord is the security; the Lord is the supply. By clutching nothing, the disciple has everything!

Father, show me what owns me. Only by clutching nothing, will
I have everything. In Jesus.

DAY 79

Salt of the Earth

Luke 14:33-34 NASB (Emphasis Mine)
So then, none of you can be My disciple who does not give up all his own possessions.

***Therefore**, salt is good; but if even salt has become tasteless, with what will it be seasoned?*

Oh, the Lord is so strange in His teachings! His subject goes from war, to possessions and ownership, to salt. And there is a "therefore"…meaning it is a connecting statement. Only the Lord can reveal His own sayings.

Salt is a substance of the earth. Salt brings out the flavor of whatever it touches. It does not seek its own flavor. *Salt* causes the flavor to snap out of those foods it touches. Salt is a needed element for all foods. Everything edible needs salt.

Life is tasteless and dull, difficult and painful. ALL of it, full of monotonous duties and cruel situations made so by the need for God on the earth.

Salt stands for the divine life, the presence of Christ that transforms ordinary living into a delightful – if taxing – adventure.

The disciple is one who is willing to lose all, live by the Cross, build the church, fight the fight (Luke 14:26-33) and own nothing… THEREFORE that one will be salt to a weak and bland world. That's why the word 'therefore' is there. The true disciple is therefore…salt.

Father, I WILL lose all, embrace the Cross when it comes, build Your church, fight the fight, and own nothing. I want to be salt. Through Jesus.

DAY 80

Salt, the Unseen Spark

Luke 14:33-34 NASB
So then, none of you can be My disciple who does not give up all his own possessions.

Therefore, salt is good; but if even salt has become tasteless, with what will it be seasoned?

The true disciple is "therefore"...salt.

Salt is the hidden substance, the unseen spark of food's enjoyment. The food is enjoyed, while the salt is forgotten. So it is with the disciple. The very presence of a disciple brings the life of Christ into the ordinariness and tragedy of life.

The disciple is the unseen force of God-Life in the midst of inertia and nothingness.

Father, I will be salt and light; not THE Salt and Light, but a vessel for You. For Jesus.

DAY 81

The Conscience of the World

Luke 14:34-35 ESV
Salt is good, but if salt has lost its taste, how shall its saltiness be
restored? It is of no use either for the soil or for the manure pile.
It is thrown away. He who has ears to hear, let him hear.

Salt was used as a preservative. It is the earliest of all
preservatives. Without salt, a thing putrefied and went
bad; with salt, its freshness was preserved.

That means that true Christianity will act as a
preservative against the corruption of the world. The
individual Christian will be the conscience of his fellows
and the Church the conscience of the world. The disciple
will be such that in his presence the atmosphere changes.

The Church must fearlessly speak against all evils, never
holding back in fear or favor of men.

Father, let the Life of Your Son be Salt in me. I will not let fear or
favor of men diminish Your influence. In Jesus?

DAY 82

For Love of the World

Luke 14:34-35a AMPC
*Salt is good [an excellent thing], but if salt has lost its strength
and has become saltless (insipid, flat) how shall its saltiness be
restored? It is fit neither for the land nor for the manure heap;
men throw it away.*

Salt was not a luxury in Jesus' time. It was a necessity
for life as both a seasoning and a preservative. Dishonest
merchants would mix the salt with sand and sell it as pure
salt. But that made the salt worthless. It could not be eaten,
and it would contaminate soil and ruin a compost heap—
"men throw it away."

How poignant is this illustration! If the believer mixes
his heart with the love of the world, if the believer lives for
self and rejects the Cross, then he loses the very dynamism
that issues from the Life of Christ. *"Any one of you who does
not renounce all that he has cannot be My disciple."*

Not only does this believer diminish his personal
relationship with Christ, he forfeits that power of influence
that changes the world. The world he prefers *loses* the Life
it needs.

*Father, I renounce all that I have and am. I will not lose You over
love for the worthless world. With Jesus.*

DAY 83

Mixture Is Wanting Something for ME

1 John 2:15-17 ESV
Do not love the world or the things in the world. If anyone loves
the world, the love of the Father is not in him. For all that is in
the world – the desires of the flesh and the desires of the eyes
and pride in possessions – is not from the Father but is from the
world. And the world is passing away along with its desires, but
whoever does the will of God abides forever.

A mixed life that wants to love both the world and love
the Lord is insipid and flat – without that strange zing of
the Lord's 'otherness.' And the disciple becomes worthless.
It reminds me of John 15: *"he is thrown away like a branch*
and withers."

I can say with deep knowledge that the Lord hates
mixture and desires complete consecration to Him. I can
say the Lord is ever after the sand of my compromise, my
mixture with the world by wanting something for ME.

How is saltiness restored? By owning/controlling
nothing. Giving up ownership and control. And by being
utterly owned and controlled by the Lord.

Pure consecration is pure joy…and a sparkling power
we cannot imagine.

Father, please reveal all the places in my heart where love for the
world is mixing with and compromising the purity of Your Life.
In Jesus.

DAY 84

The Disciple's Spiritual Purity

Matthew 5:13 AMPC
You are the salt of the earth, but if salt has lost its taste (its strength, its quality), how can its saltness be restored? It is not good for anything any longer but to be thrown out and trodden underfoot by men.

Salt stands for purity. It is made of sun and water – something from the heavens and something from the earth – but salt cannot be mixed with the sand of the earth. If it is, its purpose is ruined!

Jesus demands that His disciples carry His life as a real presence into 'the earth.' Not mere talk, not using Him to gain ambitions but His Life and His Life only. No soul.

The mixture that brings ruin to every phase of life is SOUL and its ambitions alongside spirit and its pure focus. A little soul, a portion of spirit and amazingly, *that* is disaster and futility.

The Cross takes care of the soul-ruin of the disciple and exposes the soul's unfixable wretchedness. When a group of people are (in the process of) being made pure in motive and clean of sin by the Blood, they will be a Church that affects the world.

They will be a force that exposes ungodliness and pushes back the corruption of evil wherever they move, even if only in prayer. They will also be judged, picked apart, and scorned, but where the salt of their spiritual purity is received, their influence is freedom, delight and health.

Our problem with being salt of the earth is unbelief. We don't believe that what Jesus calls for IS us, is *believers*. May we receive this salt-label with utter joy and embrace it with faith. You ARE the salt of the earth! Glory!

Father, as salt, I have the influence of freedom, delight, and health. Please dig out my unbelief so that Your spiritual purity is not obscured. Through Jesus.

DAY 85

Spiritual Ears that Hear God

We come to the end of Jesus' discourse on discipleship in Luke 14:35b —

> *ESV: He who has ears to hear, let him hear.*
> *AMPC: He who has ears to hear, let him listen and consider and comprehend by hearing.*

The 'ear' does not refer to the physical ear but to the mind of the spirit – the faculty of the born-again child of God – that is able to grasp and consider deeply Christ's words so as to obey.

Your spiritual ear is a hearing of what God reveals to you.

The Holy Spirit uses this phrase 13 times in the New Testament: *"He who has ears, let him hear."*

At the end of His teaching about discipleship, Jesus throws the matter back to us, to the realm of free choice. You can grasp or…not absorb what He offers. To 'listen' in the Greek is more than reading or hearing: it is to understand and then obey. If our hearing is not a crisis of obedience, we have not heard. We have 'read' but not 'heard.'

Hearing is the great central issue of the Christian's walk. What you hear, WHO you hear, is a matter of your life or death. Your delusion or reality. Your health or sickness. Your being a disciple or not being a disciple. All hinges on your hearing God's voice.

Jesus resisted the temptation to initiate a miracle by His absolute hold on God's voice. *"Man shall not live by bread alone but by every word that comes from the mouth of God"* (Matthew 4:4 NIV).

Father, I don't want to deceive myself. I want to be known as a doer of Your Word, and not just one who hears (James 1:22). In Jesus.

DAY 86

Fellowship with the Son

1 Corinthians 1:9 NASB
God is faithful, through whom you were called into fellowship
with His Son, Jesus Christ our Lord.

AMPC: …you were called into companionship and participation
with His Son, Jesus Christ our Lord.

As I come to the end of the great discourse (Luke 14) on discipleship, I have been much in prayer for the Lord's direction. This verse has captured my heart and amazed me.

Above all, we are called to commune with Jesus as His companion. Imagine! The Lord of the universe wants fellowship with us. Fellowship is sharing the same values, going the same way, having a heart relationship. It is dialogue, togetherness, harmony. Simple friendship— Christ always with me and I, always with Him. We are made for this…UNION!

I think of Jesus in Gethsemane, how He wanted companions to watch with Him and no one could even stay awake. In the Holy Spirit, now we can both stay awake and follow Him to the Cross, over and over. Jesus has given us the loyalty to Himself of which humanity is incapable. And it is a literal calling of the Father to *"fellowship with His Son."* May we be His friend even as He has been our dearest Friend…

Father, I've been called to this friendship with You, and I commit
to this fellowship. Make this a reality, please! Through Jesus.

DAY 87

To See the Lord

Acts 2:25 NASB
For David says of Him, I saw the Lord always in my presence…

To see the Lord. That is what impels a believer to give all, do all, leave all for the Lord. A clear seeing of Jesus is what makes a disciple. If an Old Testament man could see Him and see Him constantly, how much more could we?

To see Jesus is to follow Him. The solution to spiritual paralysis and lethargy is to behold Him.

Father, have mercy on us and open our eyes to see Jesus.

Father, I pray that the eyes of my heart, the very center and core of my being, will be opened and flooded with light! By Jesus.

DAY 88

From the Eyes of Your Heart

Ephesians 1:16-18 ESV
"…remembering you in my prayers, that the God of our Lord Jesus Christ, the Father of glory, may give you the Spirit of wisdom and of revelation in the knowledge of Him, having the eyes of your hearts enlightened…"

There is a capacity for *seeing* in the heart. To radically follow Christ is a matter of *seeing* Him. The failure to see the Lord will be the failure to surrender to Him utterly. Thousands in Israel witnessed His miracles, but the eyes of their hearts did not see the Son of God.

The religious were totally blind. Sinners saw Him from their need (like Mary Magdalene). The truthful recognized Him from the heart (like Nathaniel). And the Lord Jesus sovereignly interrupted Saul as he went, striking him blind so he could see from his heart.

Discipleship depends on seeing the Lord. To the degree you repent, to the extent you die to self – to that depth and height, you will see Jesus from the eyes of your heart and…be forever captured.

Father, I desire to see YOU. May my repentance match the level of Your desire to be seen. Through Jesus.

DAY 89

Seeing the Father

Watchman Nee from his book, *Worship God:*

"To know Him as Father is a personal relationship but to know Him as God is knowing His official and exalted standing in the universe. Many know Him as Father, but they do not know Him as God.

"What is worship? It is simply this: that I recognize that He is God and that I am but a man. When I see Him as Father, I am saved. When I see Him as God, I am finished and done with. For when we see Him as God, we can only fall down humbly and worship. The whole matter rests upon our seeing. Worship does not arise from the Blood – as precious as the Latter is: worship comes only from seeing. It does not come because we see doctrine. It is revelation.

"Praise and worship is something objective, thanksgiving is something subjective. Know the Father and the heart will be filled with joy. Know God and the heart will be filled with glory. Glory cannot be explained, but those who see God know that glory is."

Father, I thank You for Your perfect fathering of me. Now may I see You and know You unmistakably as my sovereign GOD. Through Jesus.

DAY 90

The Disciples Were Following Love

Matthew 4:20 ESV
Immediately they left their nets and followed Him.

Matthew 4:22 ESV
Immediately they left the boat and their father and followed Him.

Mark 1:20 ESV
Immediately He called them and they left their father Zebedee in the boat with the hired servants and went away to follow Him.

Why did the disciples just drop everything and immediately follow Jesus? Why did the disciples become disciples?

It's true they witnessed His miracles in Galilee. They had seen His power. But it was the personal, individual love of Christ that captured them. They loved Him because He first loved them. They felt it; they experienced the presence of a Great Love. And they followed this Source of Love. Love is the impelling force of discipleship.

Life is about love. Motive is about love: whatever we perceive as love, that will be WHY we do and WHERE we go.

The Lord Jesus would draw us out and beyond ourselves into the fathomless realm of His Love.

THAT is what makes a disciple. Not one who leaves career or family for a cause, but one who follows Love because of Love, for the sake of Love.

Miss/Reject/Refuse/Despise the Love of Christ and you will never follow radically, completely and foolishly...the Son of God.

Father, thank You that I am called to be Your disciple. I praise You that it is about love, first and foremost – not tasks, or works, or performance. In Jesus.

DAY 91

Whose Love Do You Love?

The Pharisees did not recognize Jesus because they:

- *"loved to pray...to be seen by men"* (Matthew 6:5).

- *"loved the most important seats..."* (Luke 11:43).

The Pharisees loved. They did! They just loved SELF. What you love becomes your master.

Money feels like blessing and security. Money can feed the love of SELF. There are two masters: God and mammon (Matthew 6:24).

Anyone who loves his father or mother...son or daughter more than Me is not worthy of Me.
Matthew 10:37 NIV

Amazingly, in our sinful nature, we love the darkness which hides us from ourselves – *"men loved the darkness..."* (John 3:19).

We all love. We all follow love. We will even die for what we love. The question Life asks us all is this: **Who do you love? Whose love do you love?**

Father, search my heart. Try me. Bring me to YOUR Love. I am Your disciple and I will love You with all my heart, with all my mind, with all my soul, and with all my strength! In Jesus.

A Prayer for YOU

As you read this book, whenever you read it,
just know that I will be praying for you:

Grace and Glory!

**Grace to you.
Glory to God!**

His brave (though little) rabbit,
Martha Kilpatrick

More Titles by Martha Kilpatrick

Books

Adoration
All and Only
Chariot of Fire
Altogether Forgiven

Booklet Series

Knowing God
The Great Lie
Eternal Power
Foundation of Repentance
Powers of the Universe
The Separator
Loved of God

Loving God
Seeing Him
Do You Love Me?
Marys Who Loved Him
Why Am I?
Who Do You Love?
God's Sovereignty

Hearing God
Required as Vital
Power of Decision
The Secret to Answered Prayer
The Hidden Life
The Inner Room
Consider the Lily

Individual Booklets

Surprised by God
The Secret to Fullness
Kingdom Safety
Kingdom Children

Visit Shulamite.com to access the many free online resources from Martha and Shulamite Ministries, including podcasts, a blog, daily devotions and the Martha Kilpatrick Online Library at ReadMK.com!

Shulami†e Ministries

READMK.COM
Read articles, daily devotions and more on the Online Library of Martha Kilpatrick.

SHULAMITEPODCAST.COM
Listen weekly to hear unfiltered conversations about real life with Jesus.

GETALONGWITHGOD.COM
Interested in the ups and downs of discipleship? A blog about discovering a God worth knowing.

LIVINGCHRISTIANBOOKS.COM
Shop for all things Martha Kilpatrick as well as timeless classics by those who've gone before.

THE SHULAMITE APP
Tap into all the resources of Shulamite Ministries while on-the-go with your iPhone and iPad.

Easy to use and mobile-friendly, Shulamite.com houses our ministry's latest podcasts, daily devotions, blog posts and more. Stay up-to-date on ministry news, new teachings by Martha, and all upcoming events by making Shulamite.com a daily stop!

Here is a hub for the prodigals and the truth-seekers, the brokenhearted and the hungry—all who would discover a God worth knowing!

SHULAMITE.COM

Surprisingly real, refreshingly unfiltered

The Shulamite Podcast

Check out our weekly podcast!

The joys and sufferings, triumphs and stumblings of living life as a child of God...

Come sit down with Martha, John and the rest of the Shulamites as we delight in our amazing God and discuss the practical side of discipleship from our daily lives and relationships with Jesus Christ.

**Available online at
www.shulamitepodcast.com
or through iTunes**